108 Seeds of Spiritual Wisdom

108 Seeds of Spiritual Wisdom

a quiet companion
for complex days

Gian Kumar, PhD

HAY HOUSE INDIA
New Delhi • London • Sydney
Carlsbad, California • New York City

Hay House Publishers (India) Pvt Ltd
Muskaan Complex, Plot No. 3, B-2, Vasant Kunj, New Delhi – 110070, India

Hay House LLC, P.O. Box 5100, Carlsbad, CA 92018-5100, USA
Hay House UK Ltd, 1st Floor, Crawford Corner, 91-93 Baker Street, London W1U 6QQ, UK
Hay House Australia Publishing Pty Ltd, 18/36 Ralph St., Alexandria NSW 2015, Australia

Email: contact@hayhouse.co.in
Website: www.hayhouse.co.in

First published by Hay House India, 2025
10 9 8 7 6 5 4 3 2 1

ISBN 978-93-6611-502-3
ISBN 978-93-6611-880-2 (Ebook)

Printed at Thomson Press

FSC www.fsc.org
MIX
Paper | Supporting responsible forestry
FSC® C010615

Hay House is committed to a sustainable future for our business, our readers and our planet. This book is made from Forest Stewardship Council® certified paper.

The Ink of My Soul

I don't write for praise or fame,
Nor to serve a cause or stake a claim.
I write to untangle the thoughts inside,
To give my truth a place to live.
I write to learn, to make sense of my past,
To hold on to lessons that need to last.
Even though I think I know,
There's so much more yet to learn and grow.
More to discover, experience, and realise.
Unmoved by fortune, untouched by fame.
Yet still, I write—my refuge, my mind,
A quiet home within my soul.
Not for the world, but for my own,
Leave behind my thoughts when I am no longer here.

May you, dear reader, find the moral support contained within these pages.

Preface

Although spirituality permeates our conversations and literature, we can only comprehend it superficially, and it rarely takes on its proper, deeply subjective form. In a time full of contradictions, where rapid materialism seems to prevail at the expense of deep thought, we live in an environment where many can no longer sit still—the mind keeps reverting to external signals of achievement instead of introspective awareness and a commitment to new disciplines for inner transcendence.

Pursuing outer triumphs often blocks the far more inner conquest of our minds and drives us further away from what lies within. In this time of chaos, we realise more than ever before that we must understand what spirituality means.

In my travels, I've written seven other books, establishing my ground within the domain of sacred inquiry. In the depths of life and its complexities, I have explored the vast realms of self and awareness, searching for hidden treasures beyond life's eternal mirror. Yet, I realise that these deep reflections often don't match the fast pace of today's world.

This realisation catalyses this book, which offers 108 bits of spiritual wisdom. Each of these reflections is reduced to brief insights that aim to illuminate the many facets of spirituality. My goal in sharing these short insights is to help inform readers of what it is to live a spiritual life.

This book instils profound spiritual wisdom in short reflections on key elements from each devotion, inviting readers to embrace, digest, and apply the teachings to their own lives.

We live in a world of materialism where the pursuit of worldly success is often the real, hidden idol—more worshipped than the divine! The irony is that the more we seek happiness in outside validation and accomplishments, the more incomprehensible it gets. We often measure success through external markers and ignore the internal discord that fills our lives.

Negative emotions like envy, greed, and hatred have become the prevailing passions that wriggle inside us to twist our relationships and set us at odds. In this backdrop, the need for true spiritual awakening has never been more relevant. Our awareness needs to extend beyond acquiring things and pursue something much deeper, something more enduring that brings us together with one another and with the universe.

I have not set out to write something to serve a doctrinal purpose or preach religious ideology. Instead, I hope this to be a torch—if only a small one—in our world's pale, murky darkness.

These spiritual snippets address everyday dilemmas, existential inquiries, and the ultimate truths underlying life's very essence.

They remind us that the elevated among us don't bind themselves up in the materialism of this world; they chart the way to inner knowing and self-discovery. These snippets represent divine knowledge unique to readers based on their inner needs. They are to inspire the soul, push people to their limits, open the heart, and provide respite from a wild, occasional life of chaos, rain, wind, or whatever storms may be.

Certain truths you may have instinctively known but have never articulated, and others may challenge long-held assumptions. The snippets should be read, re-read, and reflected on, but most importantly, they should be lived and experienced daily.

Spirituality is not a challenging endeavour meant only for monks, mystics, or scholars; it is an inherent dimension of the human experience. It includes self-awareness, presence, understanding, and experiencing the unity that weaves together all life. It invites us to engage with the world through wisdom, awareness, and compassion, not deny it.

This book attempts to connect life's spiritual and practical aspects while providing insights for integrating them into higher life experiences.

This collection is designed for seekers with an inquisitive spirit, those who refuse to accept things as they are, and those who aspire to delve deeper to uncover the essence of what lies beneath the surface. It is for those who wish for contentment, clarity, and clairvoyance in silence, solitude, and serenity.

Whether you read a page a day, open the book at random and seek wisdom from beyond, or read it from cover to cover in one grand explosion, I hope you find at least one nugget to hold on to help your journey towards understanding.

108 guiding lights illuminate luminosity and lucidity in this bewildering darkness. And if you do, may you reflect, recalibrate, and remember that you have a soul that desperately needs to be awakened to evolve and transform into higher consciousness.

Thank you with gratitude and sincerity,

—Gian Kumar

1

The Purpose of Life

Life is a profound personal journey to discover,
experience, evolve, and transform.
Forging relationships, embracing, and experiencing
to become healthy, wealthy, and wise.
Comprehending the ego to transcend and
revolutionise, discovers that the soul is dormant.
Righteously earn wealth to satiate desires, develop,
and transform from the material to the spiritual.
Self-discover in self-knowledge with self-experience
to realise what life is all about.
Spiritually to liberate the soul from all identifications
and attachments—*Moksha.*
Eventually, how you define, resonate, and emerge
with the purpose matters most.

2
Go Beyond

Go beyond your rational mind,
the intellect into that uniqueness of yours,
which we refer to as intelligence.
Beyond your subconscious conditioned beliefs,
that limited self of emotionally reacting
to every stimulus.
Enter the world of spiritual intelligence from
aware consciousness into spontaneous awareness
intuitively—alert, attentive, and aware
conscious of every thought, feeling, and action,
to balance the ego with the soul.

3
Beliefs

A conditioned mind, borrowed from past knowledge,
forms your subconscious section based on your
thoughts and beliefs.
Beliefs are unmindful, changing now and then
depending on what you wish to think.
Yesterday, you may have had strong beliefs
about religion; today, you may not.
Your subconscious forms your reality,
self-limiting and constraining your growth.
Enter into that super-conscious section of the mind
called the soul, witness, and introspect all you
believe to evolve and transform.

4
Transcendence

The self comprises a finite body, mind,
and the individual soul.
It remains ignorant and highly tilted towards
the material compared to the spiritual.
In the material, we compete with others
for name, fame, and wealth in egocentrism.
In the spiritual, we transcend from
the lower to the higher consciousness
to introspect and go beyond.

5

The Outer and Inner

In the outer world, we live in the duality of
happiness and sadness, good and bad,
positive and negative, truth and lies.
In the non-dual inner self, we live within the now
in silence, solitude, and serenity,
with contentment, clarity, and clairvoyance.
When we live for the outside, there is
bound to be anger, anxiety, and anguish.
But for the inner, the spirit within liberates your
mind from its bondage
of this and that towards bliss.

6
The Self

The material self is *what* you are
quantitatively to know what you have achieved.
The spiritual self is the qualitative soul of
who you are—aware and conscious
of the inner and the outer self.
We are spiritual beings
going through human experiences.
Body and mind are that material self,
the soul is that spiritual self.
And the spirit is that universal self.
All cannot exist without the other.

7

The Material and Spiritual

The material attracts
affluence and abundance.
The spiritual provides
consciousness and wakefulness.
Do not separate the two.
Life needs to live in its togetherness,
righteously in wholesomeness.
The spirit/soul does not have any relevance
without the body and mind.
Both the material and the spiritual
are requisites to life.

8

Supreme Ability

Energy has multiple abilities,
precipitating into solids, liquids, and gases,
which appears and disappears into its nothingness,
referred to as 'Shunyata'.
All that exists in the universe is energy/brahman,
which can neither be created nor destroyed.
For energy is nothing
but the ability to express its power.
The supreme ability of energy is divine intelligence.
The universal spirit that allows the individual soul
in living creatures to be aware and conscious.
Prajnanam Brahma

9
That Art Thou

It is the non-dualistic absolute nature of the universe
where all that exists is not two—Advaita Vedanta.
The creator and its creation in the ultimate
are not two.
The essence of your beingness is the same as the
quintessence of the universal spirit—non-dual.
The individual soul is at par
with the universal awareness—*Tat Tvam Asi*.
The individual soul is pure consciousness equal to
the universal spirit.
Realising this *Mahavakya* from the Upanishads
is the ultimate resolve in spiritual awakening.

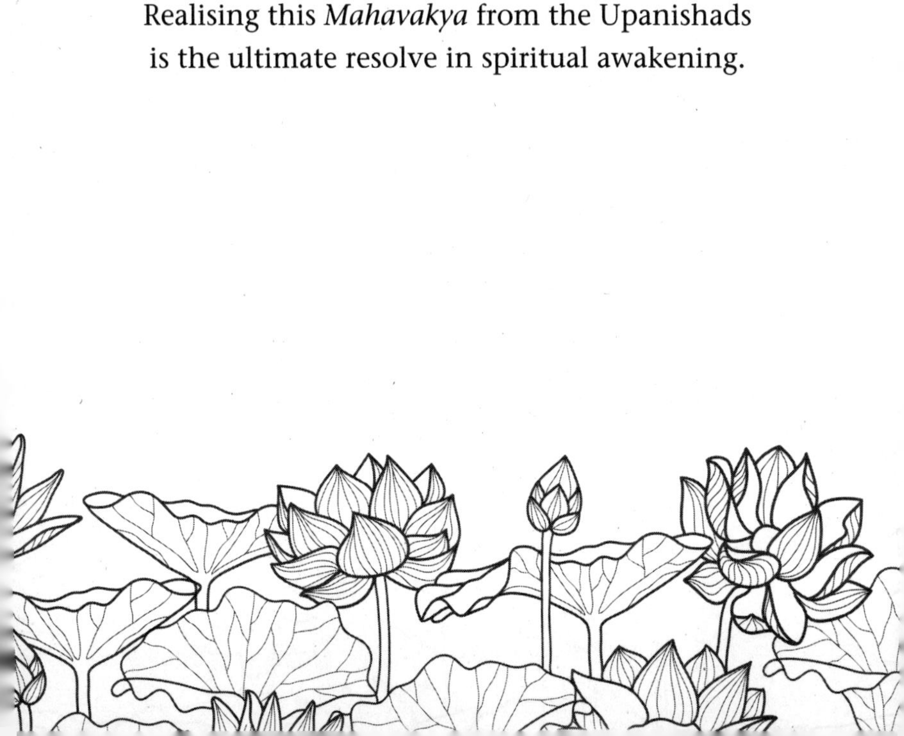

10
Intuition

Education is but a recollection of past data.
Wisdom arises from within
and not from outer sources.
Scientific knowledge for digitising information.
Enhancing efficiency by accessing data faster
through computerisation.
Simulating human intelligence to process AI.
Undoubtedly, human intelligence
will remain supreme.
Actual knowledge is spontaneous
from intuitive intelligence.
The mind transcends all conditioned processes
with instant realisation
beyond past reasoning or logic.

11
Nothingness

The universe is an expanse of spaceless,
timeless, and changeless absolute energy.
From the macrocosm to the microcosm,
the stars to the subatomic particles.
All that appears relatively in duality eventually
disappears into the universe's non-dual energy.
The fundamental, the ultimate, the manifest,
and the unmanifest are revealed as nothing
but waves of energy by science and the Vedas.
There is no bondage or liberation.
No seeker is seeking the sought,
for what we perceive is illusory,
like ripples fading back into the water.

12

Homo Sapiens

We may be proud to consider ourselves
wise human beings.
We may be proud of our art, culture, medicine,
technology, digitalisation advancements, etc.
Despite these skills, we devastate Planet Earth—from
the soil, sea, to the sky.
We destroy more than we create,
gradually making us unmindful of our finer abilities.
So, whether we are worthy of being *Homo sapiens*
requires reflection since our actions contradict
indicating beyond redemption.

13

The Soul

The body is gross energy;
the mind is subtle,
and the soul is the core.
All that exists in the universe—
an indivisible wave of formless energy.
The vital living energy is the soul,
which makes the body and mind aware
and conscious of perceiving and conceiving.
The soul is the individual self that requires only
awakening and is the source of all thoughts.
The heart is elemental to the body,
the soul is essential to the individual self,
and the spirit is the quintessence
of that universal self.

14

Hinduism

Actual name Sanatan Dharma, the eternal order,
Hinduism is neither a religion
nor does it have any founder.
It is the foremost fundamental prehistoric
philosophy depicting a holistic vision of life where
the Creator and the creation are one.
Hinduism preaches righteousness,
seeing God in everything,
and experiencing unity with the universe.
There is no duality in Hinduism; it sees God as
omniscient, omnipresent, and omnipotent
to sustain spiritedness without converting anyone
from one religion to another
or proving my god is superior to yours.

15

Aloneness

Aloneness is the state when you are alone.
Life in aloneness offers a creative opportunity
to observe, introspect, and contemplate your
random and reckless thoughts, providing a better
understanding of who and what you are.
How to self-develop?
By allowing the mind to be free from past beliefs,
conditioned by what you have
gathered from external sources.
I'm sure this little privacy of meditating in silence
within yourself, from your busy schedule,
will do wonders if you realise the value of aloneness.

16

Awareness and Consciousness

In the subject of Advaita Vedanta, spiritual awareness
is primary and consciousness secondary.
It is that pure knowing emerging through
consciousness. The supreme, primordial, non-dual
energy that creates consciousness in dualities.
You need to be first aware and then conscious.
Consciousness is to be conscious of
something in a subject-object relationship in duality.
Consciousness is the link between the individual
and the cosmos, one step less than awareness.
Awareness is the fundamental cause of everything.
There is no consciousness without awareness,
but awareness persists even without consciousness.

17

Balancing in Life

Balancing our life while living in dualities of
divine/devil, truth/lie, positive/negative, etc.,
is an art embracing both sides with
equal grace and respect.
Personal or professional, emotional or logical,
spiritual or material pursuits can be managed
righteously by acquiring wealth, satiating emotional
desires, and performing selfless deeds.
Recognising and reflecting upon our good
and evil deeds allows us to learn, grow, evolve,
and transform into higher consciousness.
We experience and realise a state of wholeness,
fostering harmony and
creating a cohesive, fulfilling life.

18

Be a Witness-er

In spiritualism,
the soul is that watcher,
the witness-er, an impartial observer.
Meaning, there are two selves settled in your mind.
The first is the mind as an actor,
and the other is the soul-spectator,
The actor thoughtfully keeps changing their role.
But then we also have the witness, as the universal
spirit, the fundamental quality of the individual soul,
to make it aware of what the mind perceives.
The witness-er, the individual soul,
comprises pure consciousness.

19

Be the Change You Wish to See

We all live in the illusions of desires,
emotions, and ego for our minds' likes and dislikes.
But there are also a few who are aware and focused.
Besides the body and mind to awaken the soul.
The mind is an interplay
between the ego and the soul.
Awaken the soul to watch your thoughts constantly.
Change can happen when you change your mind.
Always be alert, attentive, aware, and conscious.
Not imprisoned by those desirous thoughts.
Constructive changes occur with courageous choices
to confront, contend, and capitalise on every change.

20

Be Who You Are

Embrace your true self, the spirit within the soul.
Be alert to what you are in the body and mind.
You are bound and conditioned by your mind,
taking you on a roller-coaster ride
of this and that.
Be free from all those compulsions of mental
conditioning that has been going on for centuries.
Be authentic, bold, and free.
When you let go of all that you are bound,
your third eye opens beyond
race, religion, and rituals
to discover your uniqueness.
So, please be free to be who you are,
content, calm, and clear, creating a
meaning and purpose in life.

21
Beliefs

Your conditioned mind, formed over centuries,
provided by others, creates beliefs that totals
your subconscious mind.
Beliefs are unquestioning, changing occasionally,
depending on what you wish to think.
Your subconscious structures the mind
in lower consciousness and is self-limiting,
restricting your innovativeness
and preventing you from exploring something new.
Negative beliefs encompass
anger, anxiety, and agony.
Enter that super-conscious section of the mind,
which we call the soul,
and be watchful of what you believe to overpower
them with innovative thoughts.

22
Change

Life is a constant dance of change.
The only permanent factor in life is change.
Changing now and then for something
new to emerge.
Embrace change, for growth is nothing but change.
Nothing lasts, changing from moment to moment.
We are spiritual beings going through
ever-changing human experiences.
Freshness and newness are requisites of life,
where change is imperative.
After knowing this fact,
be thoughtful and responsible
for our ever-changing thoughts, feelings,
beliefs, actions, and circumstances
with grace and respect.

23

Cause and Effect

Nothing happens in isolation;
every action has a reaction.
Every cause has an effect; every effect has a reason.
One cannot indeed exist without the other.
Every thought, good or bad, has an outcome.
The cause may be in your control, but not its results.
So, do your duty, and do not be attached
to the fruits of your actions.
As you sow, so shall you reap.
They are two sides of the same coin.
It is not mechanical but philosophical to perceive
and grasp what existence is all about.

24
Creation and Destruction

The physical reality is an illusion;
the ultimate existence
are energy waves within which
we temporarily exist as particles of energy
to appear and disappear.
Upanishads declare there is
neither creation nor any destruction.
No seeker seeking any sought;
there is no bondage or liberation.
The ultimate reality
comprises eternal nothingness.
Hindus refer to it as Shunyata.

25

Shunyata

Shunyata is a Sanskrit word originating in
Hinduism, which defines zero.
Designating the formless, eternal,
infinite nature of the universe.
A void from which creation appears to
disappear back into its nothingness.
In the silent, dark energy of nothingness lies the
potentiality of everything.
Advaita Vedanta declares all that exists
in eternity is Brahman. The rest is an illusion.
It is identical to what quantum physics
today declares as energy.

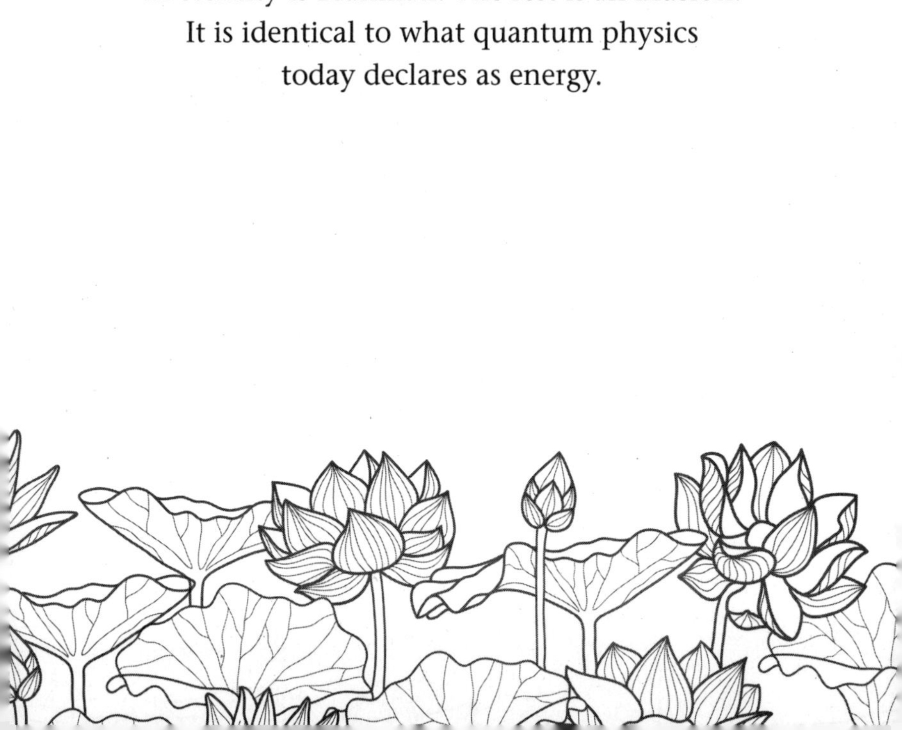

26
Happiness

Happiness is a positive emotional state of mind.
You can be happy as you are or happy when
you get something you want.
It always has a shadow of sadness lurking behind it.
One can be wealthy and unhappy
or poor and yet happy.
The mind is always satisfied by
being dissatisfied; never happy for long.
To be happy, be who, what, where, and as you are.
Without any regret, remorse, or repentance.
Evolve and transform; do not run after
that transient happiness.

27

How to be Spiritual?

To be spiritual is a personal inward journey
to go beyond body and mind to awaken
the third element we refer to as the soul.
Transcend from lower to higher consciousness.
Observing your reckless monkey mind and
its thoughts, operating from
past and future conditionings.
Focus and concentrate on the now.
Self-reflect on your thoughts, feelings, and actions.
Meditate from moment to moment to be mindful
to know, experience, and realise,
beyond the body and mind,
who and what you are—the spirit.

28
Maya

Maya is that veil of illusions
that makes us believe the unreal is real.
It is a play of the mind
to trap in emotional desires
to identify and attach.
An intoxicating cosmic force of energy
that creates a field of materialism.
The infinite appears finite,
the eternal-temporal, and the nondual-dual.
Binding the soul to an egoist world of a false
'me and mine'.
Taking us away from
divine consciousness towards selfishness.

29
The Imprisoned Soul

The soul is pure, non-dual consciousness,
and on par with spiritual awareness.
It gets confined within the body and mind
to experience the dualities of this and that
to realise what life is about.
The mind, in turn, binds the soul to its
desires, emotions, and attachments.
Imprisoning within its cognitive walls,
separating in an egoistic illusion of pleasure and pain
in the lower consciousness.
Spiritual freedom materialises when the soul awakens
to experience its true identity after dissolving the ego
with a silent mind to embrace that we are
spiritual beings who go through human experiences.

30
Inner and Outer Self

The outer self is the ego-self with lust and greed,
with unquestioning beliefs and attachments.
Imbalanced, mostly in anger, anxiety, and anguish.
Unless you remove that veil of Maya,
confining the divine residing within,
your soul remains separated within the mind.
The actual inner self is that spirit, the witness.
Soul is that witness-er,
aloof from your body and mind.
The mind creates your personality—a false persona.
The soul creates your individuality—uniqueness.
The outer self is bound to name and gender.
The inner self is that boundless, formless spirit.

31
Limitations of the Mind

The mind primarily functions for it's me and mine
for its desires and emotions.
It operates in relativity with the duality of
hot and cold, positive and negative, divine and devil,
truth and lie, etc., for its likes and dislikes.
It primarily functions by thinking from the past,
going into the future, bypassing the present.
The mind persists with unquestioning beliefs,
constantly chattering randomly and recklessly
multitasking into this or that,
rather than being focused and centred.
The human mind is 80 per cent negative,
and around 98 per cent of the mind
functions subconsciously in lower consciousness
for selfish needs.

32
How Do You Live Well?

The Law of Diminishing Marginal Utility
states that satisfaction and joy reduce
as consumption increases.
So is the case with money and materialism.
Materialism has surpassed spiritualism to such an
extent that instead of harmony and peace,
we are heading towards ruination, wanting more
and more than we can utilise.
We require the balance of both—
material for happiness, spiritual for inner peace—
to realise a meaningful purpose in life.
Living not for perfection but for
moderation and balance.
Having values that resonate with
spiritual awareness and simplification.

33
Logical Thinking

Every thought connects to the
past, projecting that into the future.
We apply logic for reasoning
to analyse any situation,
seeking an outcome that suits us personally.
Our selfish ego, beliefs, and emotions also interfere
in our logical reasoning with hidden motives
of: 'What's in it for me?'
Unless we balance our rationality
with spiritual intelligence, logical thinking
will remain imbalanced in self-interest.

34
Religion vs Spirituality

Religion takes you towards an external god.
Organised and structured towards
doctrines and dogmas.
Mythical, mythological, and mystical.
Religion is communal; spirituality is individual.
Religion separates; spiritualism unites.
Religion is regressing; spirituality is transcending.
Spirituality takes your mind towards the inner self.
It is a metaphysical subject of life where you are that
God, Guru, and the Self—That art Thou.
To transcend and transform towards peace of mind.
Connecting the universal spirit
with the individual soul.

35

Who Is This 'I'?

The 'I' within me is a deeper exploration
of the essence of my existence beyond
what I call my body and mind.
When I remove all external identities of my gender,
name, and attachments, I am that witness with the
ability to watch my thoughts, mind, and body.
Then, 'Who Am I?'
Since all that exists in the universe is energy
transforming from waves to particles and back.
I am that supreme ability of energy, settled in the
mind through spiritual awareness.
I am that divine intelligence, *Prajnanam Brahma*.
I am that spirit to explore, discover, experience,
and consciously comprehend and realise
all we know of the inner and the outer.

36
Why Is Spiritualism Imperative?

The Second Law of Thermodynamics proclaims
that energy moves in entropy—disorder.
Likewise, our thoughts move randomly,
recklessly here and there, multitasking, neither
focused nor centred towards the actual values of life.
We require spirituality to comprehend
the meaning and purpose of life,
for that contentment, clarity, and clairvoyance;
for that, silence, solitude, and serenity,
not to identify and attach to the outer.
Be proactive and not emotionally reactive,
but be intuitively aware of every moment,
for that interconnectedness with all that exists,
inner peace, and emotional balance to acquire
self-knowledge, experience, and self-realisation.

37
Reincarnation

Incarnation refers to energy
manifesting into a physical form.
On the other hand,
reincarnation is a repeated cycle of birth and death.
Reincarnation is a controversial topic in
science and philosophy.
It suggests that the soul transmigrates into a different
body after death until it realises liberation
from its bodily karmas.
In spiritualism, the soul is that
metaphysical pure consciousness that
neither incarnates nor reincarnates.
Reincarnation is a personal religious belief
without proper evidence to prove or disprove.

38
Self-Observation

It is a practice of becoming aware and conscious
to examine your thoughts, feelings, and actions
in the present.
Observing yourself unquestioningly,
witnessing your experiences impartially.
It is the foundation of spiritual growth
to cultivate self-awareness through mindfulness.
It helps you recognise how your inner mind
emotionally reacts desirously to the outer world.
It is more about understanding your body and mind
through the soul in a better manner.

39

Spiritual Atheist

Atheism is the denial of God in any religious belief.
A spiritual atheist offers respect to all gods
but follows none.
He has no belief in people
wearing turbans, robes, long beards, etc.
To be spiritual is to awaken that sleeping soul within.
He lives in the moment, and meditation is his life.
He sees divinity in all, in divine deeds
for the sake of divineness.
He participates and balances
the material with the spiritual.
He transcends into a higher consciousness through
constant introspection, reflecting in self-observation.
For him, contentment and clarity
are far more critical than unquestioning beliefs
in mythical and mystical fables of religion.

40

Spirit and Soul

We are a composite unit of three energy abilities:
Body (gross), mind (subtle), and soul (core).
The spirit is that supreme ability in the form of
universal aware energy.
Immersed as the universal witness
within any individual soul.
Spirit is that divine force creating
a field of pure consciousness.
The individual soul is a witness-er
of the body and mind,
making the mind aware and conscious
of all it perceives.
Awareness is the non-dual essence of the spirit.
The basis of all knowledge manifests in every
perception, the cause of all-knowing and existence.
The soul sustains individuality,
while the spirit is that cosmic connection.
The soul is that link between
the individual and the universal spirit.

41
Spiritual Invocation

You call upon your inner spirit to invoke,
say a prayer
for guidance, blessings, and wisdom
from a higher force.
When you evoke, it awakens the soul.
When you invoke, you surrender;
when you evoke, you awaken
the spiritual awareness towards
higher consciousness.
Spiritual invocation involves an appeal
to the universal spirit in humble submission.
But when you evoke, you worship emotionally,
say, in distress, depression, or fear,
Both complement to summon through
appeal and practice,
calling upon that divine spirit residing within
to awaken the soul
to activate the mind towards that divinity
in divine deeds for that divineness
of who and what we are a part of.

42
Spiritual Wisdom

Spiritual intelligence is divine.
It is that ability to understand with clarity the
knowledge of who we are beyond
the body and mind.
Maintain a certain balance and order between the
inner and the outer, regardless of any situation.
After applying spiritual intelligence to experience
its potentiality, we realise spiritual wisdom
existentially through contentment,
clarity, and clairvoyance.
From self-discovery through self-awareness to
self-experience self-realising, for all that exists
is merely waves of absolute energy vibrating in
different frequencies in solids, liquids, and
gases, or as matter and consciousness for the
souls to experience and enjoy the dualities of life
while we exist.
Therefore, spiritual wisdom
is the integrated realisation balancing
the material with the spiritual.

43

Divine Connection

All successful people are alert, attentive, and aware.
They do not follow others, transcending
beyond their mental capacity
into intuitive intelligence.
To be a follower is an easier way out,
an escapist route to copy, imitate, and gossip in ego.
All religions demand you follow their dictums,
creating a psychological genesis
of separatism and hatred.
Parents, teachers, gurus, societies, and politicians
demand that you follow them.
Over 98 per cent of people are followers,
and around 2 per cent are leaders.
Most of the wealth is held by
merely 2 per cent, more than the total wealth
of the remaining 98 per cent,
because most of us are followers of this or that,
devoid of divine connection.

44

The Animal Nature

A human has three states of living—
animal, human, and divine.
We are midway between the god and the beast
within the spiritual and the material.
We are unique due to the presence of consciousness,
which allows us to transcend toward divinity.
However, most of us do not know about
the soul and spirit and how to experience them.
Despite all the multiple intelligences,
from existential to cosmic,
the net result is that we are destroying planet Earth,
unconsciously, in a beastly manner.
Unless we re-evaluate our education
towards the spiritual self,
we will eventually use science and AI for destruction.
Regrettably, none of us is concerned about this.

45

What Is AI?

Artificial means fake, and intelligence is divine.
Intelligence is spontaneous, intuitive,
Instinctive, and innovative—
generating fresh knowledge from
the inner and outer.
AI is a powerful computing tool,
neither intelligent nor advanced.
Processed by recollecting and
recombining past data,
it is merely a sophisticated extension
of past human intellect.
It can logically generate, simulate,
imitate, and mechanically reproduce.
Authentic intelligence is spiritual
and original, stemming from mindfulness;
centred in the now to explore, discover,
and conceive God and the universe.
Prajnanam Brahma—Intelligence is Divine.

46

The Conditioned Mind

Conditioning of the mind has been prevalent
over centuries, based on dictates set
by the government, society, religion, culture,
community, and customs,
defining how we perceive, think, and behave.
Even our truth is biased towards psychological
repetitions imposed upon us
from media to educational systems.
From birth to death, we obey and follow to maintain
a prescribed order, either through fear of religion,
laws by governments, or social pressures.
When you free yourself from this cage, you discover
more than what your conditioned mind tells you.
Breaking psychological imprisonment is a
prerequisite for any spiritual awakening.
You cannot imprison love or force yourself to love.
To observe, experience, and creatively realise, you
need to rise, not fall, in love.

47

The Power of Choice

Dualities in life provide the power of choice.
Choose between this or that
for your likes and dislikes,
Life is a flow of energy for us to choose
between the correlative duality.
Creating destiny reveals the quality of our lives.
All your thoughts, decisions, and intentions—
whether falling in love, desire, or emotions.
Meaning, you choose before you begin to act.
Our choices can make or break us.
Remember, you are what you are today
because of the choices you made earlier.
Live consciously despite any dilemma or uncertainty.
You always have the choice to design your destiny.

48

The Power of Faith

Faith is a strong energy force, creating
a field of inner strength with hope and resilience.
It is based on personal and emotional beliefs,
expressing hope beyond the
rational, conscious mind.
It instils hope during challenging times, providing
confidence to move forward despite
unfavourable circumstances.
It is that intense belief to pursue
what you feel is right,
trusting yourself even while facing setbacks.
It is deep and personal,
transcending even without tangible proof.
Since it goes beyond all beliefs, we must be careful
about whom and what we have faith in.
Therefore, always keep your mind open to every
opinion, feeling, and belief, eventually becoming
faith, making you rigid in what you believe.
Lastly, have faith in your self and your capabilities,
more than anything else.

49

The Power of Intention

When your mind zooms into what you deeply desire
and intend, you forcefully resolve how to put your
thoughts into action.
If your mind is centred, focused, and clear, the
power of that intention can change your life.
Intention is consciously concentrating on a strong
mindset to experience and manifest what one desires.
It is the determination of what
you think and believe.
Your deeds depend upon the degree
of your intention.
The clarity behind intention brings forth
the willpower of that zeal,
the inner strength of your determination.
The intention is single-pointedness
to what you desire.
So, clearly define your intentions,
focus on the present, and constantly ensure
they align with your goals to transform and evolve.
Intention alone is not enough;
it also requires vigour, vitality, and vivacity.

50

The Quality of Life

You need not wear a saffron robe
or paste ash on your forehead.
There is no need
for any colourful thread on your wrist.
Nor any robe, turban, or beard
to falsely project who and what you are.
Simply balance your life righteously
with the material and the spiritual.
Along with your duty towards the law of the
universe in unity, wholesomeness, and selflessness.
Always be observant of your intentions and attitudes
to remain clear and calm in all situations.
Observe to learn, understand, and act consciously.
Express and exhibit equal grace and respect for all.
Prioritise physical, mental, social,
and spiritual health.
Pursue moral passions, gratitude, and financial goals.
Propel and prompt towards
a holistic life mindfully.
Placidness in both
normal and abnormal situations.

51

Absolute and Relative Truth

The absolute truth is subjective,
unchanging, and eternal—ultimate
and not bound to anything like the sky.
It is universal and constant, beyond space and time.
The actual or ultimate truth is
as it is now and forever.
However, we also have relative truth—flexible
and prone to change.
Relative truth can alter over time,
like facts based on individual perceptions,
interpretations, and explanations.
Both facts and relative truths arise
from observed and experiential reality.
The absolute is the ultimate reality,
realised through spiritual awakening, transcending
all human cultures, social constructs, and periods,
representing the true nature of the universe within
which all that exists appears to disappear.
Absolute love, truth, God, and reality
remain in perpetuity.

52

The Ultimate Reality

We live in a physical reality that we can
observe, perceive, and measure.
Science, as yet, is not able to confirm the ultimate.
But in the Theory of Quantum Mechanics,
scientists claim: All that ultimately exists
in the universe
are vibrational energy waves,
turning into particles and back into waves.
Ancient Advaita Vedanta,
on the subject of non-duality,
declares that physical reality is an illusion, Maya.
The ultimate is the source behind many
and the many behind one—Brahman or energy.
Possessing the ability to appear and disappear.
Superimposing on the substrate of its
fundamental, ultimate reality.
Spiritual awareness is the supreme ability to make
the mind aware and conscious.
In meditation, the soul awakens and transcends
towards this ultimate spirit.

53
What Is the Spirit?

Both quantum physics and Advaita Vedanta agree
That physical reality is but an illusion—Maya.
All that ultimately exists at the submicron level
is nothing but waves of energy
or the spirit—Brahman.
The subject of spiritualism elucidates
that you are neither the body nor the mind
since you can self-observe, read, and observe both.
The spirit is who you are—Awareness.
The body and brain are the manifestation
of what you are.
To be spiritual is when you transcend
within the mind,
towards that awareness—the authentic self.
The purpose of the soul is to make the mind
aware and conscious.
Transcending the mind towards that actual self—
spiritual awareness residing in the soul.

54
What Is God?

God is omniscient, omnipotent, and omnipresent
in everything as absolute non-dual energy waves.
God is that supreme ability of energy present in the
human mind as spiritual awareness.
Aware-conscious energy that allows us to perceive
and conceive the dualities of life.
God is that transcendent being beyond
space and time, we call the universal spirit.
The spirit settled as the witness within an
individual soul to observe its mind.
When we consider God, a noun with a name
and a gender, we downgrade Him.
But when you conceive Him as a verb, a spirit, that
divine energy flowing in divinity through your
divine deeds for the sake of that divineness,
you are—That art Thou—Shivohum.

55

Sakshi Yoga

As long as the mind is there, we live in
the relativity of this and that for both
body and mind in duality.
The soul inside, however, persists in non-duality.
The divine state exists within our deeds of divinity.
So, we are that divine;
we don't need to *become* divine.
We must transcend our minds towards higher
consciousness—the soul as the witness-er.
We have five primary yoga classes in that direction:
Karma, Bhakti, Jnana, Raja, and Sakshi.
Sakshi emphasises the supreme ability of energy
as the witness.
Observing through the soul via
aware, conscious energy as the witness-er of
one's thoughts and actions constantly without any
identification nor attachment
is what we call Sakshi Yoga.

56

The Soul

The body is gross energy; the mind is subtle,
and the soul is the core.
The essential divine energy is that spirit
within the soul,
which makes the mind aware and conscious of
perceiving and conceiving.
The soul is that individual entity that requires only
awakening and is the source of all thoughts.
The heart is the source of the body
The soul is the essence of the self.
Spirit is the quintessence of the universe.
The soul is that state of pure consciousness—Turiya,
The spirit—TuriyaTitta—is Shiva
in absolute awareness.
This ultimate state incorporates non-duality,
Advaita, where the separation in duality
is but an illusion—Maya.
To play the dual role of the divine and the devil in
body and mind—Lila.

57
Role of the Soul

The soul is that seat of individual consciousness that
differentiates between the living and the non-living,
making the mind and the body alive and conscious.
Spiritual energy is the supreme ability that makes
the mind first aware and then conscious of what it
gathers from its sensory organs to perceive.
The first role of the soul is to make the mind
conscious of all it perceives.
The second role is to
observe the inner flow of thoughts,
remaining uninvolved and unquestioning.
The third role is to spontaneously provide
fresh bouts of aware energy, which we call intuition.
The fourth role is the responsibility to
create every living creature unique
and different from all others.

58

Spiritual Sex

Spiritual sex is the conjoining of two souls,
fostering a sense of unison in sacredness.
Physical sex is the union of two bodies
for pleasure and reproduction.
Psychic sex is more about want and lust.
In spirituality, two bodies conjoin
in orgasmic oneness,
totally in the now, meditatively demonstrating
non-duality—Ardhnarishwar.
In the body, sex is an interplay of sensual enjoyment
and reproduction in duality.
Transcend in sex with purity for the sake of oneness
between two separate life forms.
It is that creative force of life energy
seeking unity for continuity.
Do not abuse, suppress, or become obsessed with sex.
It is the pathway to physical, psychic,
and spiritual unity.

59

Sensitivity

Sensitivity is how responsive you are
to the environment.
How you feel and think of all that you perceive.
When you are emotional about
your likes and dislikes,
you become selective and sentimental.
Say, when you love someone and
expect the same in return,
it reveals selfishness in sentimentality.
However, when your love is
unquestioning and selfless,
You are aware, attentive, considerate, and sensitive
to others' feelings.
Intuitive, empathetic, and dispassionate towards
humans, animals, and plants, to all that exists.
To be sensitive is to proact; sentimental is to react.
Sensitive people do not feel positive or negative.
Spontaneously attach to all that exists
in unity with love, grace, and respect.

60
Worry

Worry is a form of repetitive negative thinking
centred on future outcomes and events.
Yet many a time, worrying while facing problems
brings about positive results.
Life today demands a lot from us;
often inviting worry.
Many of us are overly concerned about
what others will think.
Live in the present, and plan for tomorrow;
do not worry.
Concentrate, contemplate, and challenge
what you worry about.
Practise deep breathing and mindfulness.
If you are not careful, worries can lead you to
anxiety and depression.
So, watch and witness your worry.
Otherwise, worries may invite pessimism and fatigue.
Be spiritual, entering into higher consciousness to
balance your excessive negative thoughts
with positive ones.

61

Spiritual Requisites

Contentment

It is the first indicator towards a spiritual journey,
seeking a deeper meaning and purpose
in life as a goal.
Go beyond the material self in selflessness.
After you are content with whatever you have.

Clarity

You are free from doubt and distractions.
You are free from ego with purpose and direction.
When you know who you are beyond body-mind.
You self-reflect on your desires and weaknesses.

Mindfulness

Concentrate, contemplate, meditate, and introspect
as a witness-er to your thoughts, beliefs, and actions,
taking the mind into higher consciousness.

Clairvoyance

Go beyond intellectuality spontaneously to be
instinctive, intuitive, and intelligent, which we refer
to as the 6th sense or the third eye
to perceive spiritually.

62
Dispassion

First comes passion, an intense and uncontrolled
feeling of what you desire.
Then, we have the compassion to feel for others in
empathy and understanding,
Last is dispassion—a spiritual flow of energy when
you do not identify, nor attach to your emotional
feelings and are sensitive to all as one.
Mahatma Gandhi exemplifies dispassion, selfless
love, care, and respect for all.
In passion and compassion, the mind connects to
past and future emotions,
In dispassion, you are sensitive,
not sentimental—in the now for all.
Dispassion involves equanimity, rationality,
and fairness without being influenced
by external circumstances.

63

The Human Mind

The mind is an electromagnetic flow of energy released by chemical activity in the brain, carrying information through neural pathways via neurons, connecting the conscious, subconscious, and superconscious sections as a composite unit in the brain.

The superconscious section is in pure consciousness and is also called the soul.

It is responsible for making the mind aware at any given moment. The conscious section focuses and thinks after being aware of any dual factor, either hot or cold.

Then we have the subconscious mind functioning in auto mode from memory and reasoning, consuming over 98 per cent of the mind's neural activity, functioning in relativity—randomly and recklessly, desirously multitasking in selfishness.

The superconscious is intuitive, the conscious focused and centred,

whereas the subconscious is random in lower consciousness for likes and dislikes.

64

Intelligence Is Divine

Ancient scriptures pronounce 'Prajnanam Brahma'
as the first *Mahavakya,* meaning a great saying.
The supreme ability of energy or Brahman is
intelligence—how we know and understand from the
microcosm to the macrocosm through intelligence.
Of all that we know, learn, and discover
about the universe.
The intensity of intelligence differs from
one individual to another, depending upon how
awakened our soul is to check and guide the
cognitive mind from running amok in illusions of
this and that.
Understanding through perception, memory,
intellect, discrimination, and consciousness is a
result of our spiritual intelligence.
The Vedas proclaim that the spirit manifesting
through intuition, instinct, and intelligence is the
foundation of all knowledge that our scriptures call
Parabrahman, Parmeshwar, or Paramatma—beyond
all other abilities.

65

Spiritual Consciousness

Today's world is obsessed with material consciousness and pretends to be spiritual, not knowing anything about the spirit, soul, and the meaning behind being spiritual.

We live in a lower consciousness, which we call the subconscious. We remain in ego or subconsciousness, not knowing of the higher soul.

Only when the cognitive mind is silent does the soul awaken to elevate into a state of awareness beyond materiality and physicality.

Spiritual consciousness is that inner realisation, the need of the hour to save our planet Earth.

Spiritual consciousness uses the mind as a tool rather than being used by it.

Associating with the soul and the spirit is the essence of going beyond the material realm of duality.

Recognising the absolute non-dual, the creator and its creation are the same.

66

Organised Religion

There is a strong disconnect between
organised religion and the youth of today
who refuse to believe and follow supernatural fables
to human gods telling them how to live.
The belief in human gods is
gradually being replaced by
quietly sitting alone, meditating, and
introspecting the inner self,
learning and experiencing how to live righteously.
Self-knowledge to discover the self, inwardly
transcending, evolving, and transforming
makes far more sense
than unquestioningly following
or worshipping exhausted beliefs and practices.
Gradually, educated people also realise that we fear
God more than we love Him.
That is why, mainly out of fear or want,
many of us follow a religion,
entering into further ignorance.

67

Spiritual Path

We are overly dependent on outside sources for what we learn and experience, making us forget that there is one journey where you are on your own.
No master, guru, or God can take you there.
They can only show you the direction.
The spiritual path energises after you awaken the dormant soul going inwards.
It begins after discovering who and what you are beyond the body and cognition.
Always remember you are that God, guru, and the self.
It is all about self-knowledge, self-awareness, experiencing, and realising the authentic self to lose your identity and attachments in selflessness.
Experience and recognise that the divine resides in your divine deeds in divinity.
Theoretical knowledge will only make you a follower of some god, guru, or sage.

68

What Makes You a Leader?

Leaders have curious and doubtful minds.
They are satisfied by being dissatisfied.
They are intuitive, intelligent, and instinctive.
They are not mechanical,
nor do they give up quickly.
Always alert, attentive, and aware.
Leaders do not follow any given path.
They create their path for others to follow.
Leaders are fearless, whereas followers are engulfed
with fear and insecurity.
Leaders doubt and question, coming out afresh,
whereas followers simply believe.
Leaders are responsible and accountable for their
acts, whereas followers pass the buck to others.
Leaders dream and act intelligently.
They inspire and guide others
to achieve higher goals.
Leadership is the ability to empower, direct,
and influence others.

69

The Inner and the Outer

The seen and unseen, the physical and
metaphysical—Mind, body, and soul
Yet you remain incomplete?
Because you have a fair amount of knowledge about
the body and mind, and none about the soul.
The inner self is that spirit of who you are,
the witness of your body and mind
through your soul.
The outer is that false mask of your personality that
you project to others quantitatively.
The inner is that uniqueness, the qualitative self.
Both cannot exist without the other.
Yet the mind remains ignorant
of the inner—soul and spirit.
Synchronise and balance the inner with the outer
For that, fulfilment and completeness
are in wholesomeness.

70

Am I a Nobody?

Yes, I am a nobody.
Also, I'm not.
I am something in my
identification and attachments,
living in this transient material egocentrism.
Spiritually, I am a nobody in the nothingness of the
universe to appear and disappear as a non-entity.
All that exists in the universe is the wave of formless
energy in unity and continuity,
representing nothing in eternity.
When your mind realises you are nothing,
the ego dissolves, and the soul
becomes free from its imprisoned cage.
Celebrate life fully, living in the present.
And not emotionally, for its past and future.
To leave behind your uniqueness, a legacy,
when your body and mind
are no longer here or there.

71

Spiritual Master

God, Guru, and the self are the same.
In the concept of Vedic non-duality,
all that exists is not two.
Experiencing and realising the inner self—
the spirit is supreme.
God is the source and the essence of all creation.
Omnipresent, omniscient, and omnipotent.
Guru is that link, the external manifestation of God,
making the seeker recognise the unity of all.
Upon spiritual awakening, realise you are that
God, guru, and self.
Body and mind are what you are, and the guru is
that mirror showing who you are,
none other than 'That art Thou'.
Self-inquiring, experiencing, and realising all that
eternally exists is the only supreme ability of energy
to play its Lila (drama) in Maya (illusions)
through spiritual awareness.

72

Be Yourself

All living beings are unique.
You are here to exhibit and express your uniqueness.
The outer self expresses your personality.
The inner self exhibits its individuality—
physically, mentally, and spiritually,
seeking self-knowledge to experience self-realisation.
Be alert, attentive, and aware of your thoughts,
feelings, and actions.
Intellectual knowledge borrows from here and there.
Conditioned by others through beliefs,
making you a follower of this and that.
Your intuition, instinct, and intelligence
mature your individuality.
Follow not others but the inner witness-spirit via
the soul watching through its body and mind.
All three fuse into a single,
composite individual unit.

73

Fear

The mind persists in the prison of fear.
The higher the fear, the higher the insecurity.
The source of fear deeply connects with your
identification and attachments.
Connected to the future, we have anxiety,
a form of fear.
Connected to the past, we have agony.
Since the mind is never present, it keeps rotating
from the past to the future.
Love is that antidote to fear.
Selfless love without any expectation abolishes fear.
Do not try to run from fear.
Simply watch and witness.
You will be able to tackle fear much better.
Fear makes your mind react in uncertainty.
Fearlessness is godliness; the one who goes
beyond fear is in total freedom.

74
Mindset

A spiritual mindset focuses on inner growth,
dissociating from religious or mystical beliefs.
It emphasises a universal approach, balancing the
material and the spiritual.
Living in harmony with a greater sense of fulfilment.
Connecting to that higher power
of the universe—spirit.
Prioritising life with introspection and mindfulness.
Practising inner awareness, compassion, and love.
Perceiving a flow of energy that connects to nature.
Letting go of egoistic identifications
and attachments.
Understanding the meaning and purpose of life
means knowing *who* you are beyond
your body and mind.
Concentrate, contemplate, and meditate for the
clarity of *what* you are.
Constantly alert, attentive, and aware of the
inner and the outer.
Cultivating a mindset empowers us to conquer
obstacles and achieve goals.

75

Being-ness

Being-ness is the essence, the reality,
and the actuality of who we are.
It refers to that intensity of existence when you
recognise *who* you are as the universal spirit.
Going through human experiences
guided by your soul, transcending the body
and mind of *what* you are.
All that exists in eternity is only that being-ness in
formless waves of energy—the supreme ability—
in the nothingness or Shunyata of the universe.
Spiritual beingness proposes that your
fundamental essence is eternal and divine.
As the governing energy, the spirit makes the mind
aware and conscious.
Being-ness or the spirit is that aware wakefulness that
differentiates the living from the non-living.

76

Spiritual Power

It is that being-ness or spiritual awareness from
which all existences appear and disappear.
Spirituality defines limitless power
as absolute energy, the potentiality of all
relative/kinetic energy in motion.
It refers to that qualitative state of having existence
emphasising the awareness of everything and an
intrinsic understanding of the 'is-ness' of being.
Spiritual power is supreme, infinite, eternal,
spaceless, timeless, changeless, and limitless energy.
It transcends all material, religious, and psychic
beliefs of this and that in relativity.
Hindu Mahavakyas state—Aham Brahmasmi.
You are that highest aware-conscious energy.
That art Thou—Tat Tvam Asi.

77
Harsh Realities

We constantly look outside for answers,
even when the kingdom of God is within.
As we age, beauty fades away; we become weak,
gradually leaving behind everything we embrace.
Nothing is perfect—society, religion,
community, government, or education;
otherwise, the world would have been better.
Negativity is far more prevalent than positivity.
The ego personality overshadows the individuality.
Guru's motivational speeches are of little help,
for anxiety, anger, and anguish persist.
Meditation, jaap, t'ai chi, Zen, or prayers, too,
have not worked for most as claimed.
Grabbing, snatching, and clinging to attach and
accumulate is the mantra of today.
Wolves in sheep's clothing—because
the soul is asleep.

78
Energy

All that exists in the universe is formless,
non-dual absolute potential energy waves in unity
and continuity—eventually resulting in nothing,
which our scriptures call
or zero—unmanifested energy.
But what is energy?
It is the ability and power to interchange
in subset forms to work effectively.
Human intelligence has learnt how to renew energy
from one form to another and use it for work.
Matter and consciousness represent
10 per cent of the universe;
the remaining is dark matter and energy.
The supreme ability of energy makes living creatures
aware, which is highest in humans, to explore and
discover all that we know of the universe.
Aware energy retains its eternal nondual state
in the form of instinct, intuition, and intelligence
from which we spontaneously observe
and become aware of all we know
to think, perceive, and conceive.

79
Non-Duality

Non-duality is a philosophical concept
that states there is only one ultimate reality,
which is changeless, timeless, limitless, and eternal,
within which all relative existences
appear and disappear.
Science refers to that as energy.
Non-duality remains indivisible and can neither
be created nor destroyed, having multiple
interchangeable abilities, of which the supreme
ability is non-dual awareness.
It enables the discovery within the mind
of all we know of the universe.
Non-dual means there is
no subject-object relationship.
The creator and the creation are the same.
The rest is all an illusion created by the senses,
perceived by the mind to exhibit and express that
which is ephemeral, for the eternal remains as
nothing but energy.

80
Awareness

In the spiritual realm,
there is no existence in physicality,
only the presence of eternal waves
of non-dual Brahman
exhibiting temporary presence in matter
and consciousness, in duality,
to appear and disappear back into
its metaphysical absoluteness of nothingness,
which quantum physics calls energy.
Awareness is the supreme ability of energy.
Hinduism calls the same as divine intelligence—
Prajnanam, Parabrahman, Paramatma,
or Parmeshwar, which enables all living creatures
first to become aware and, after that,
conscious of all that they perceive
and conceive in a subject-object relationship,
functioning in duality from its
power of consciousness.

81

Past, Present, and Future

Time is a relationship between
space, time, and motion.
It is a flow of now, from one moment to the next,
segregating into chronological, psychological,
and biological duration,
depending upon any individual experience.
The past was once present,
and the future will be the present.
The present is endless
since the past and future are just mind concepts.
Learn from the past and plan for the future,
but remain focused on the present.
A life where your mind is balanced;
allocate 10 per cent for past thoughts,
20 per cent for the future,
and 70 per cent reserved for today,
for it is impossible to live 100 per cent in the present.

82
Limitations of the Mind

The human mind, according to science,
is 80 per cent negative and 90 per cent repetitive.
The mind survives on ego, predominantly on its
identifications and attachments.
It subconsciously functions over 90 per cent in
autopilot from its memory and intellect in lower
consciousness, jumping from past to future,
bypassing the present.
Thoughts move randomly here and there.
Recklessly multitasking into this or that
and destructive if left unchecked.
Primarily, the mind is based on emotional beliefs,
making you selfish and prejudiced,
and the soul remains asleep within the mind.
What you see, feel, and think also changes over time.

83

Self-Belief

The mind survives and functions on
three essentials—desire, belief, and intentions.
Without belief, the mind has no desire to experience.
Beliefs are unquestioning,
based on outside knowledge
gathered and borrowed from here and there
into this or that in ignorance.
However, when a belief emerges,
and you are in doubt,
question and use your intelligence,
whether you should believe or not.
Self-belief is that confidence, an internal insurance,
established in self-awareness that creates a mindset of
your ability to perform.
It activates positive energy, overpowering your
setbacks, an essential part of success
in your personal growth.
Therefore, always listen but do not believe easily.
Doubt and question to create
that clarity in self-belief.

84

The Art of Life

The art of life is how we discover, create,
and manage our thoughts, feelings, and actions.
How should we navigate with self-awareness and find
harmony in the meaning and purpose of life?
Adapt to whatever comes—good or bad,
positive or negative, happiness or sadness—
every moment with equal grace and respect.
Respond to every stimulus proactively and with
intelligence, not in a reactive manner.
Make the most out of every moment,
Mindfully keeping your mind
alert, attentive, and aware.
Observing every thought, feeling, and action
to awaken our souls, seeking balance and fulfilment
with creativity and gratitude
to go beyond the clutches of desires and emotions
of 'me and mine'.

85

Liberation

How do we liberate the soul
from the clutches of the mind?
First, you must understand that
the body, mind, and soul
are the quanta of what you are,
and spiritual awareness is the quality of who you are.
The mind has been conditioned
over centuries by outside forces,
bound to its identification and attachments to
desires and emotions for its likes and dislikes,
for self-preservation.
When you silently observe, experience,
and realise—you are not the mind.
The soul awakens in the superconscious section,
remaining uninvolved, unaffected, and liberated
from what we identify and attach,
which is me and mine.
The soul upholds, becoming free
from the ego's limitations, and
sustains its state of pure consciousness.

86

Be Centred

Centring of the mind means being calm and focused,
balanced and fully present in the moment.
Focused on the here and now, having complete
control over your thoughts.
Centring is to balance the material and the spiritual.
The soul awakens when the mind is centred and
silent in meditative awareness—spontaneously
observing inside out without any thoughts.
In random thoughts, the mind vibrates recklessly
here and there in this and that for
its likes and dislikes selfishly.
Be centred and focused so the soul can check and
guide the mind intuitively and instinctively.
Such an inner state of intelligence
makes the mind dynamic and fresh.
When body, mind, and soul conjoin—centred, clear,
content, and calm—it celebrates life mindfully.

87
The Spirit

Advaita Vedanta claims all that exists is a state of
non-dual Brahman—absolute and wholesome as
waves representing nothing but energy.
Spirit is that supreme ability of energy—complete,
eternal, infinite, spaceless, and timeless,
with the ability or the power to exhibit and express
many interchangeable forms of
matter and consciousness,
which appear to disappear into nothingness.
Spiritual energy is metaphysical, opposing
physicalism; humans possess this supreme capability
residing within the superconscious section of
the mind, which we call the spirit and soul.
Spirit is that aware energy that makes the soul
spontaneously conscious to make the mind
intelligent and mindful of all we perceive and
conceive of the divine, universe and the self.

88
The Universe

All that exists in the universe is absolute energy,
from which a network of subset energies in
the form of matter and consciousness
appear to disappear.
The eternal remains only as waves of metaphysical,
non-dual infinite energy, spaceless and timeless,
complete without any beginning or end
that cannot be created or destroyed,
remaining indivisible.
This eternal, absolute energy also has the
supreme ability to make all living creatures
aware and conscious.
Humans have the highest energy—spiritual
awareness, enabling us to
perceive every existence consciously.
Our scriptures refer to this supreme non-dual ability;
aware energy—the eternal, absolute, ultimate reality.
All other realities are temporary and prone
to change within limited space and time.

89

Work Is Worship

Worship has two significances.
The first is to pray to a
deity with religious rituals and dogmas.
The second is how we respect, honour, and dedicate
ourselves to our work and duty righteously with a
steady and calm mind.
Sincere devotion to one's work equals dedication to
the divine with divinity in divineness.
I would say the second is a true worshipper.
A steady mind requires two essential aspects:
Contentment and clarity.
When you are content, the mind stabilises
to perform your duty, which benefits one and all.
You are more centred and focused with clarity of
your thoughts, feelings, and actions
rather than multitasking selfishly into this or that.

90

The Human Mind

Our scriptures tell us that the mind continues to
operate in a state of illusion, presuming what it
perceives and conceives in its subconscious or
lower-conscious section to be authentic and accurate.
The reason for illusions is that
there is no reality in deep sleep.
In dream sleep, when one wakes up, reality vanishes.
In the waking state, reality keeps changing within
space and time from the real to the unreal,
as per the mind's comprehension.
The mind remains in an illusion,
revolving in the relative duality,
managing life between good and evil.
The real you is that state of spiritual awareness,
which awakens the soul only when
the mind is alert, attentive, and aware,
making it conscious of all it perceives and conceives.

91
Fulfilment

Fulfilment in life is realised when
one transcends from the material towards
the spiritual in a balanced manner.
When you are awake, aware, and conscious to
create that meaning and purpose for your life.
When you constantly watch and witness
your thoughts flowing randomly and recklessly
here and there to check and guide your mind
as and when required.
When you transcend from desires and emotions
into the realm of humility
with humanity in humanness
to accept every favourable and unfavourable
circumstance with equal grace and respect.
When your body, mind, and soul
unite for that wholesomeness.

92

Past and Future

The mind is but vibrations of energy in
different frequencies flowing in past thoughts,
projecting that into the future,
bypassing the spontaneous moment of the now.
All three—yesterday, today, and tomorrow—are
measurements of those movements in that
psychic energetic field.
Potential energy remains in order,
whereas kinetic energy creates disorder.
Kinetic energy cyclically vibrates for creation,
destruction, and recreation.
What creatively contributes are those moments of
that existential now—from one moment to the next.
So, do not worry anxiously about yesterday
or speculate about tomorrow.
You are wasting those precious moments of now.

93

Live without Regret

Live life to its fullest to discover
the meaning and purpose of life.
It is human to err;
every failure is a stepping stone to success.
Follow your path, materially and spiritually.
Go with the flow—observing, experiencing, realising,
and accepting successes and failures,
happiness and sadness with equal grace and respect.
Regret will unnecessarily raise stress
and may create depression.
Any regret should teach: Do not make
the same mistakes again.
Celebrate life without regret or remorse,
experiencing life with your third eye open—
alert, attentive, and aware.

94

Our Education System

The modern education system is more of a failure,
disintegrating into destruction,
being quantitative rather than qualitative,
destroying planet Earth
from soil, sea, to air.
The mind gets conditioned into patterns established
by institutions, society, governments, and religions
based on past knowledge.
It takes away the freedom to create and discover.
Producing intellectuals with fancy degrees in
egocentrism from the past and borrowed knowledge.
The true purpose of education should be
to extract spontaneous intelligence in
every student innovatively
to discover fresh knowledge intuitively for the
material and spiritual aspects of wholesome living.

95
Mental Pollution

The aggressive force of mental pollution is
affecting and impacting human health
and the environment.
Anxiety, stress, and excessive negative thinking,
combined with environmental destruction erodes
the social fabric, destroying the ecosystem.
The mind overly goes towards sex, violence,
jealousy, lust, and greed.
We are mentally more destructive
and less constructive.
The Foundation of Science claims
the mind is over 80 per cent negative.
The Second Law of Thermodynamics states
that every form of energy moves in
disorder, losing quality.
Our essential mindset desperately requires an uplift
if we wish planet Earth to survive for our
well-being—physically, mentally, and spiritually.

96

The Spiritual Path

First, we will need to know
about the spirit and the soul.
To know who we are beyond the body and mind.
Since we can observe, read, and direct our minds.
We are spiritual beings going through
human experiences.
The spiritual path begins after we awaken the
soul to make the mind aware and conscious
from one moment to the next, inside out.
It is an ongoing journey throughout life where
all three bodies, mind and soul, interact with each
other, playing their respective roles.
The spiritual path begins when the mind is silent.
The soul awakens the material and spiritual.

97

Moksha

Spiritual moksha translates as liberation or freedom.
From identifications, accumulations, and
attachments, blinded by the material world.
The Vedas provide four goals for leading a proper life.
Dharma, Artha, Kama, and Moksha—righteously
acquire wealth to satiate your desires and, after being
content, liberate your soul imprisoned in your mind.
Cultivate mindfulness and self-awareness.
Be a constant witness, an impartial witness-er
to your thoughts, feelings, and actions.
Gradually, become non-attached
to the activities of the mind.
Then, you see the world without any illusions.
You no longer cling to your desires and
emotional thoughts—free and liberated.

98

Matter and Consciousness

In the infinite expanse of the universe,
all that exists is nothing but energy waves.
In the physical and metaphysical forms,
matter and consciousness appear to
disappear and return to nothing.
Matter and consciousness are expressions
of the same reality—Brahman/energy.
Awareness is the ultimate and the supreme ability
of energy to make the mind
first aware and then conscious.
Awareness is subjective; consciousness is its objective.
Matter is a form appearing as solid under observation
through consciousness.
Within the mind, the subconscious
is the cognitive mind.
Conscious is the focused and centred mind.
The superconscious is spontaneous, intuitive,
and pure—the Soul.

99

Mind vs Spirit

The mind moves in duality, here and there,
multitasking into this and that, for it's me and mine.
The spirit remains non-dual, residing in the soul.
The soul awakens when the mind is
observant and silent.
The mind clings to its
identifications and attachments.
The spirit is for that unity in all.
The mind is intellectual; the spirit is intuitive.
The mind is a follower of its beliefs.
The spirit creates uniqueness.
The mind thinks, feels, and experiences.
The spirit is that witness,
and the soul is that witness-er.
All three are essential for the mind to experience
the divine and the devil.

100

Doubt

We live in a world rampant with
unquestioning beliefs,
making us followers of this and that
of what others want us to believe.
Doubt is the force of energy towards
better understanding.
It is a virtue not to be a blind believer,
allowing you to be more fluid,
question, and improve.
Doubt is necessary because neither philosophy
nor science is perfect.
Doubt is the foundation of scientific inquiry.
Since beliefs are not compulsorily bound to truth.
Doubt arises, questions spring forth,
and you learn more and better.
Always remember, doubt is necessary for you
to use your inner intelligence.

101
The Ego Mind

Ego is the unconscious belief of claiming who
and what you are, creating a false self.
Constantly trying to prove 'I am superior.'
Ego is essential for material growth to counter and
challenge competition to conquer.
The ego remains erratic and imbalanced,
always wanting more and more.
Unless you go beyond materiality into spirituality,
where your persona, that false mask, is reduced.
The soul awakens for you to experience and realise
who and what you are beyond your body and mind.
When you love from the mind
and think from the heart,
it dissolves the ego to awaken your soul,
to experience that authentic, spiritually aware self.

102

The Art of Balance

Life is all about balancing this and that,
here and there.
Whether at work, at home, or with friends.
Both success and wisdom demand a balance between
the physical, mental, and spiritual.
For experiencing anything, the mind requires clarity,
consistency, to be conscious, calm, and in control
You need to walk on this tightrope,
balancing with a balanced mind
since all aspects are significant—health, wealth,
spiritual, social, emotional, or financial.
So, balance is the key to what life tells you.
Do not try to be a jack of all trades
and master of none.
You cannot know everything, but you can create
that balance between everything.

103

Spiritual Wealth

One is rich from what he is rather than what he has.
You may have plenty of health, wealth,
family, and friends.
Without spiritual know-how,
there will always be something amiss.
For a wholesome living of physical,
mental, and spiritual.
All three are essential to have a proper balance.
Physical and mental provide quantitative results.
Spiritual well-being shall
bestow qualitative awareness.
Today's world is replete with anger, jealousy, greed,
and anxiety, devoid of spiritual wealth.
The spiritual journey begins after you are content
with those ever-demanding material wants,
seeking meaning and direction in life,
to know who you are beyond your body and mind,
to lead a fulfilling, wholesome life.

104
Spiritual Knowledge

One who goes on a path of self-discovery
to experience self-awareness beyond body and mind,
to balance material life with spiritual experiences
after knowing the subject of spiritualism.
When a seeker wishes to comprehend this knowledge
with clarity, away from myths and mystics.
All that exists is Brahman,
also claimed by quantum science.
The spirit is eternal, formless energy waves that never
incarnate or reincarnate.
The supreme ability of energy from which the mind
discovers everything in the universe.
The seeker must procure spiritual knowledge
to know who you are as the spirit
to awaken the individual soul.
The conscious mind then experiences
the spirit of life.

105
Spiritual Seeker

A spiritual seeker goes on the path of self-discovery
and self-awareness beyond body and mind.
Spirit is that universal, eternal, non-dual awareness
that makes the mind first aware and then conscious
of perceiving and experiencing.
Spiritual knowledge is for that seeker who wishes to
comprehend, experience, and realise.
Who and what you are beyond the body, mind, and
the individual soul.
The spirit is that supreme ability from which the
mind comprehends the mysterious universe.
Despite having all material wealth, health, family,
and friends, there will be something amiss
unless the seeker knows how to experience
the true self, the Spirit.

106

Reality

Reality is that which is seen and also unseen.
Indicating that physical reality emerges when
consciousness interacts with quantum possibilities;
a mental construct based on neural interpretations.
Reality is a complex subject involving multiple
perspectives within the intersection of objective,
subjective, scientific, and spiritual connotations.
Unseen factors like consciousness, dark matter, and
energy remain a part of reality even though not
directly observable or comprehensible by our senses.
Reality can be both illusory in material forms and
transcendent in spirituality.
Suggesting that reality is fundamental,
contextual, and transcendental.
The ultimate reality is that substrate within which
all transient realities are superimposed.

107

Mental Chatter

The mind constantly chatters into this or that,
here and there, from past thoughts into the future.
We live in that mental chaos, with the
mind persisting repeatedly in negative thoughts,
randomly and recklessly in ego.
Check and guide your monkey mind through self-
talk and self-observation to become self-aware.
Watch and witness your thoughts as they go astray.
Reduce fretting about the past or
fantasising about the future.
Be in the present.
Do not unconsciously react to desires and emotions.
Live for today and go with the flow.
Be alert, attentive, and aware
of your chattering mind.
Learn from yesterday, plan for tomorrow,
but live for today.

108
Intellect vs Intelligence

Intellect is that realm of thoughts for discerning, determining, and deducing acquired knowledge.
Meanwhile, intelligence arises from self-awareness, the spontaneous ability of the mind to receive fresh impulses via instinct and intuition.
Intellect utilises borrowed knowledge from memory for reasoning collected from here and there.
Meanwhile, intelligence discovers fresh knowledge and understanding with clarity.
Intellect is mental; intelligence is spiritual.
Intellect provides the knowledge to know something.
Intelligence is for understanding that knowledge.
Intelligence is divine, from which you discover, from subatomic particles to stars, all we know of the universe today.

'The gateways to wisdom and knowledge are always open.'

Louise Hay